Ziggy and Zelda Laugh their Heads Off

Written by Helen Baugh
Illustrated by Simon Bosworth

Collins

Ziggy and Marley sat having a chat,
talking of this thing and talking of that …

... when Marley remembered a dream from last night.
"Oh, Ziggy! Please picture this most awful sight!
I dreamt of a dinosaur. It was so smelly!
I wanted to run, but my legs turned to jelly."

"Your legs turned to jelly? What flavour was it?

Was it shiny and smooth? Did you try a small bit?"

"Not *real* jelly, Ziggy! My legs just felt shaky.
I was scared, so I froze and my legs felt all achy."

"Oh, you were SCARED! Well, that sounds a bit like the first time I learnt how to ride my big bike. I tried to be brave (but I wanted my mummy). I even had butterflies inside my tummy."

"Butterflies in your tummy? Are you sure that's true?

They need air to fly in. They can't fly in you!"

"Not *real* ones, Marley! My stomach just felt quivery. I was nervous – my tummy felt fluttery and shivery."

"Oh, you were NERVOUS! Well, that's no surprise.
You'd want to take care with a bike of that size.
My new puppy, Titch, likes to run by my wheels.
From the moment we met, I fell head over heels."

"You fell head over heels? Your new pup made you fall?

You poor thing! That's awful, with a pup who's so small!"

"Not a *real* fall, Ziggy! I did not trip up. It means that I felt full of love for my pup."

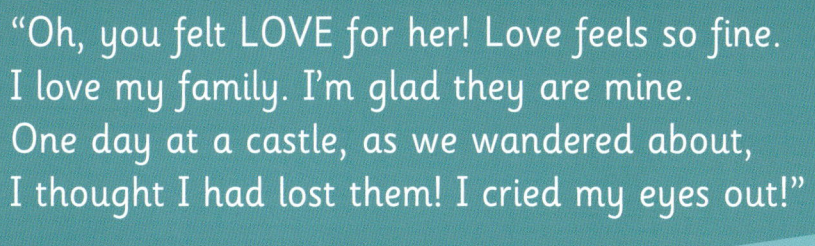

"Oh, you felt LOVE for her! Love feels so fine.
I love my family. I'm glad they are mine.
One day at a castle, as we wandered about,
I thought I had lost them! I cried my eyes out!"

"You cried your eyes out? How did you see?

Did it hurt? Did they bounce? Could it happen to me?"

"Not *really* out, Marley! I just cried and cried. I was so upset, there were no tears left inside."

"Oh, you were UPSET! I'm pleased you're okay.
Eyes on their own would look funny, anyway!"

The friends shared some giggles.
They laughed on and on …

... till they both laughed their heads off ...

... then they put them back on.

23

Spot the clues

Ziggy and Marley use sayings to help them explain how they feel.
Sayings can be confusing the first time we hear them!

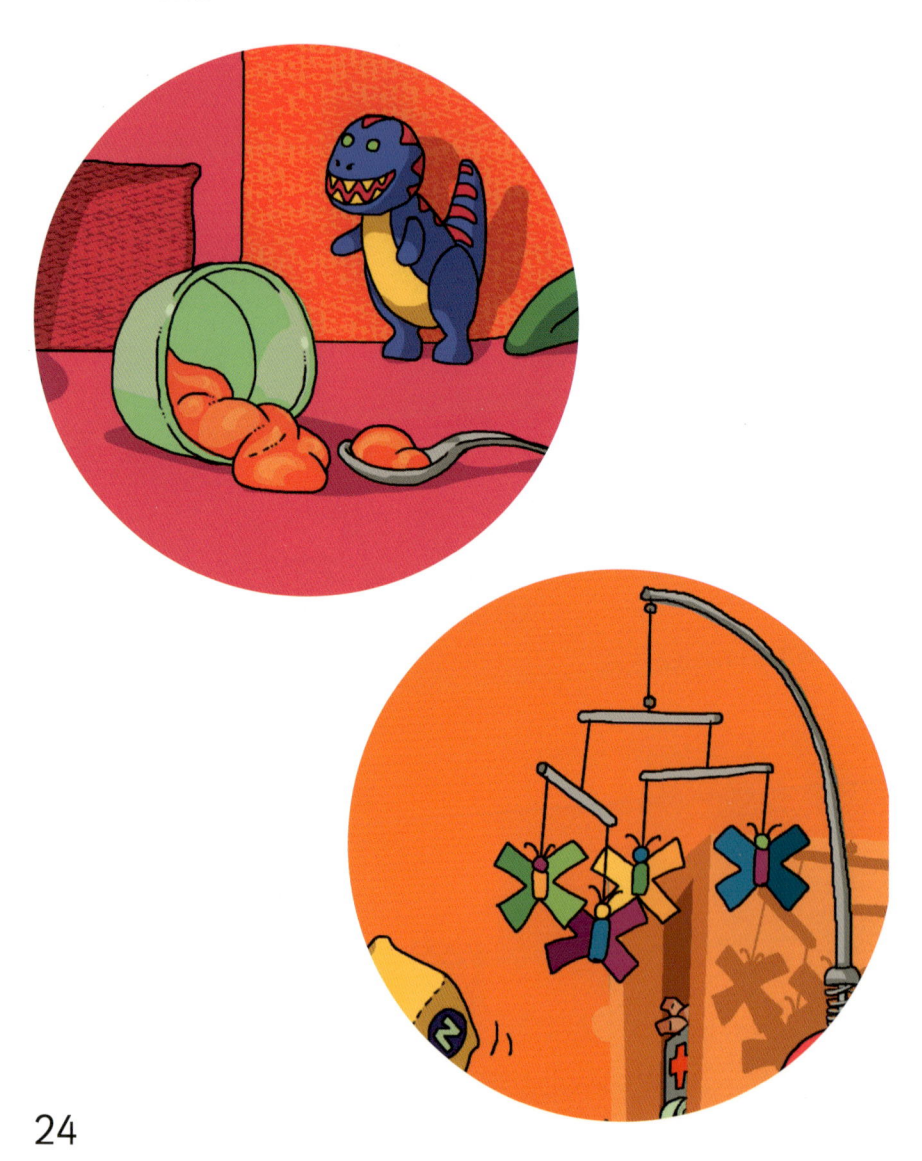

Some objects in the pictures link to the sayings they used.
Can you go back and spot them?

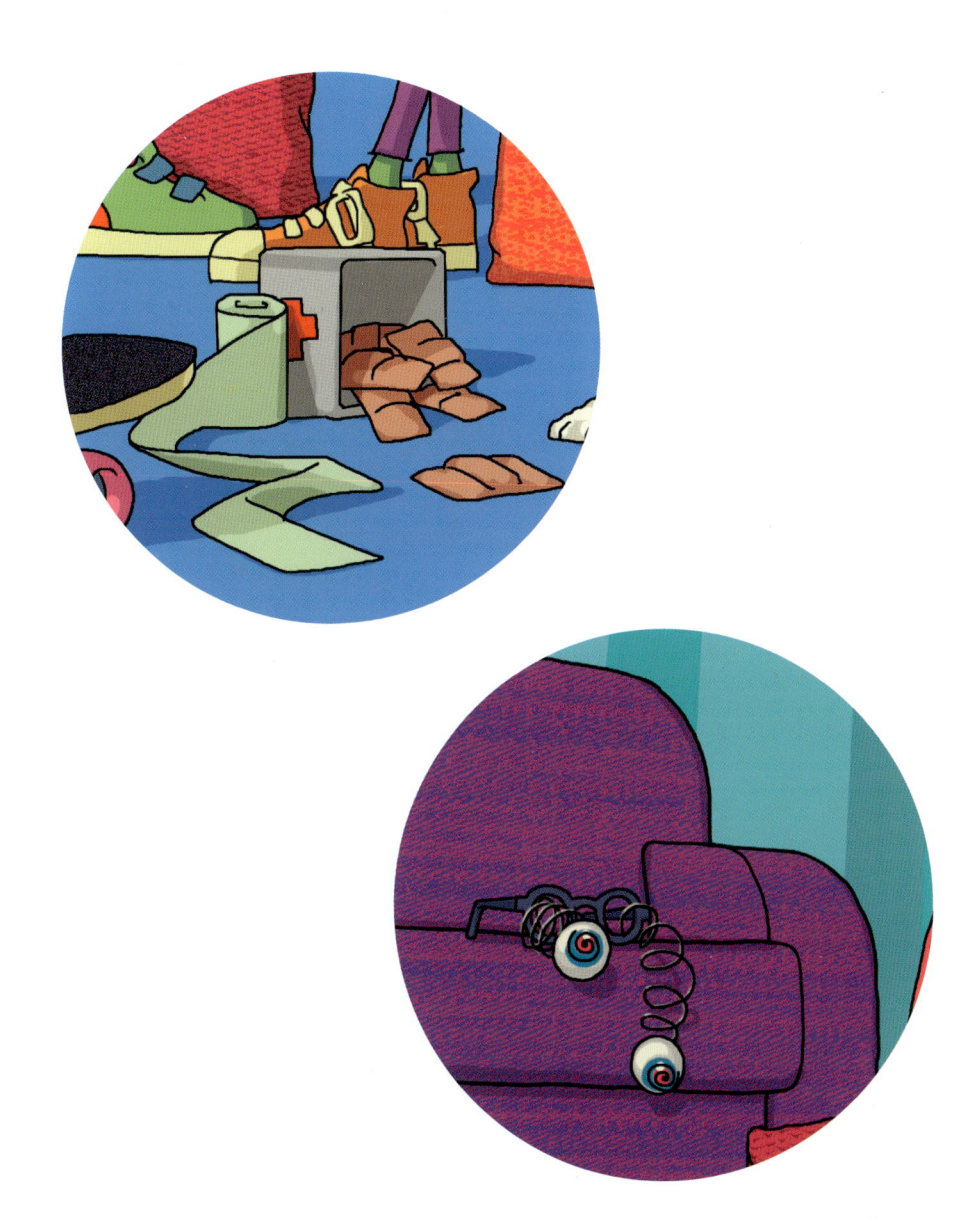

25

I say, I say, I say …

What would happen if you swallowed caterpillars?

Yuck! Would I be sick?

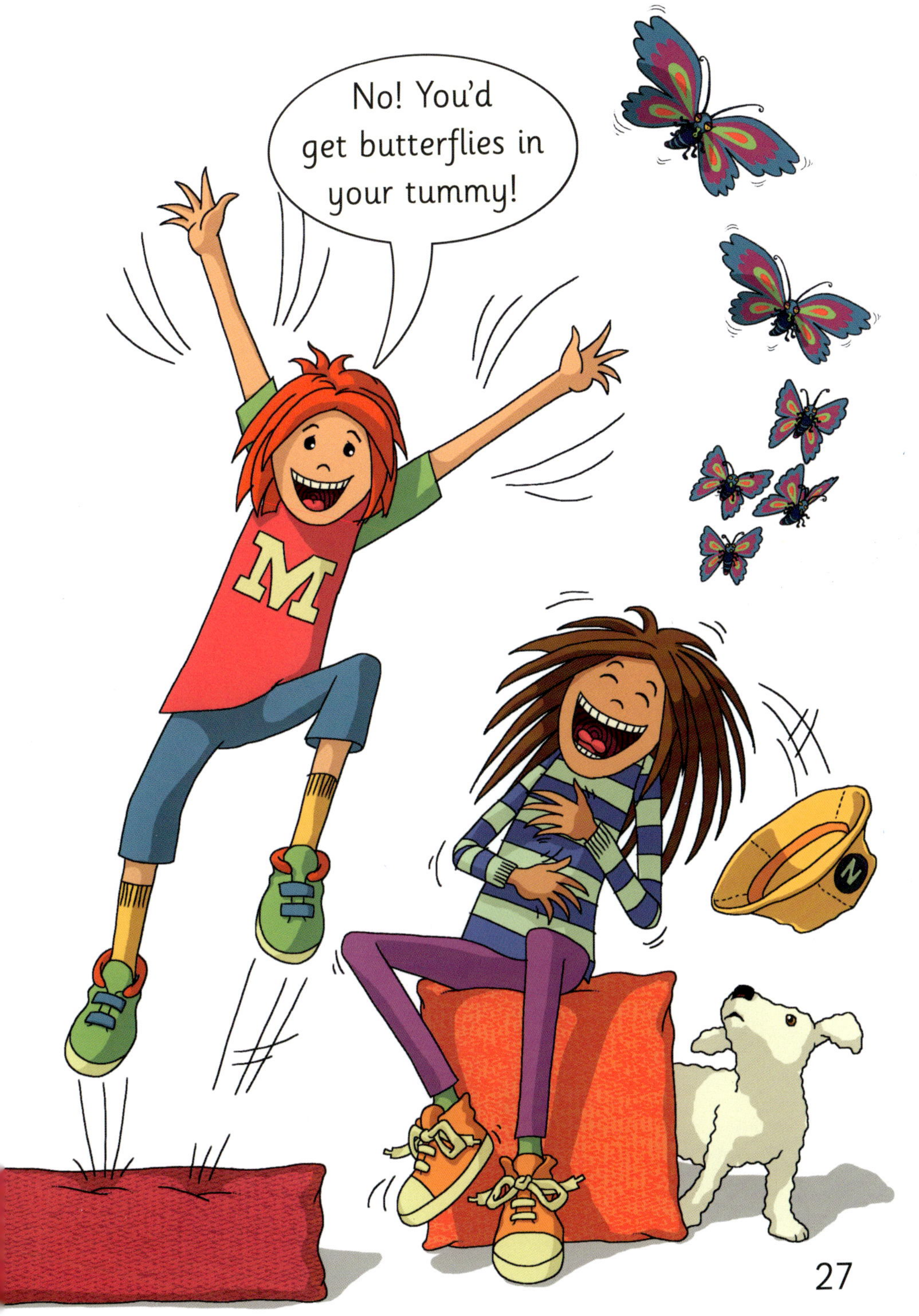
No! You'd get butterflies in your tummy!

I say, I say, I say …

"What goes: ha, ha, plonk?"

"I give up. Tell me. What goes: ha, ha, plonk?"

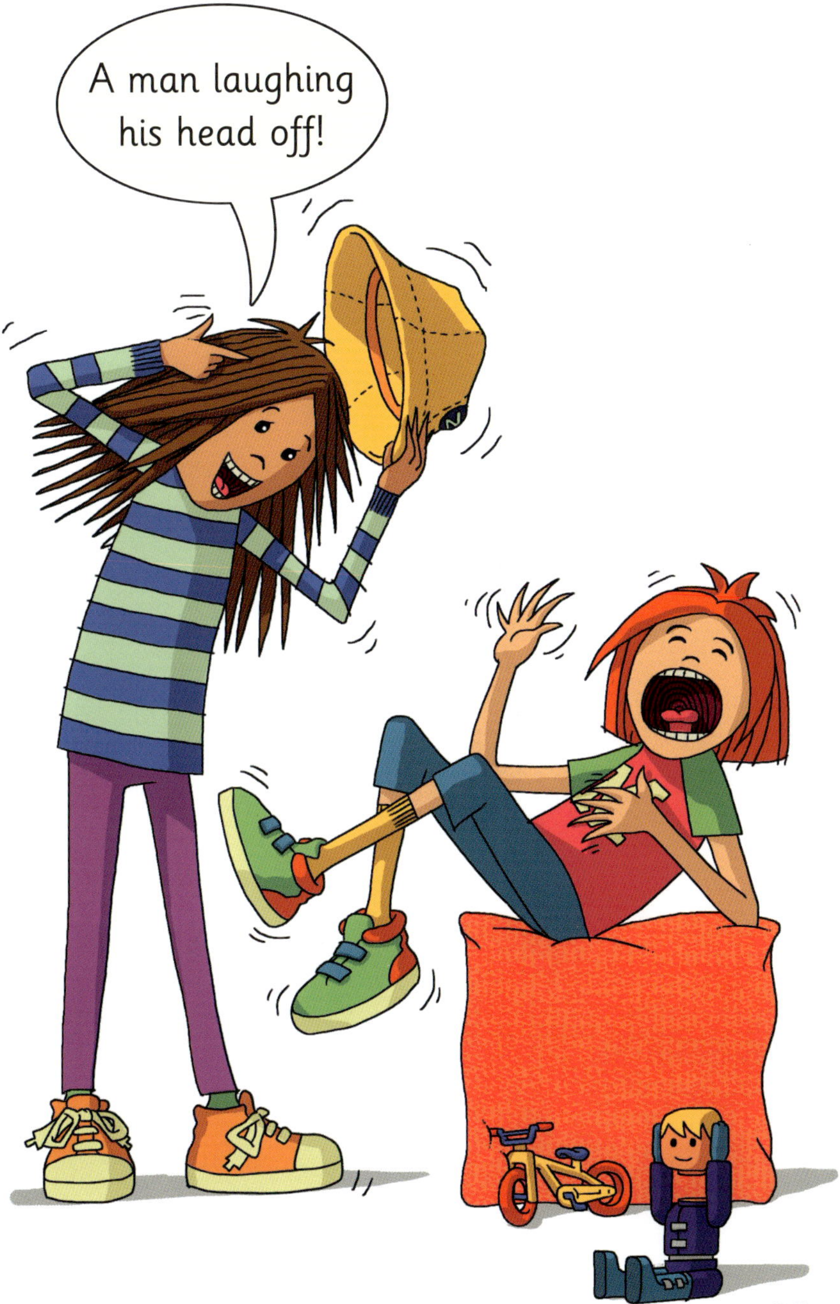
A man laughing his head off!

What a chat!

I had butterflies in my tummy.

I cried my eyes out.

30